PAKISTAN
the culture

Carolyn Black

A Bobbie Kalman Book

The Lands, Peoples, and Cultures Series

Crabtree Publishing Company
www.crabtreebooks.com

The Lands, Peoples, and Cultures Series

Created by Bobbie Kalman

Coordinating editor
Ellen Rodger

Production coordinator
Rosie Gowsell

Project development, photo research, design, and editing
First Folio Resource Group, Inc.
Erinn Banting
Tom Dart
Greg Duhaney
Söğüt Y. Güleç
Jaimie Nathan
Debbie Smith

Prepress and printing
Worzalla Publishing Company

Consultants
Dr. Naeem Ahmed, Vice Consul, Consulate General of Pakistan, Toronto; David Butz, Department of Geography, Brock University; Nancy Cook; Tahira Naqvi, Westchester Community College and New York University; Dr. Naren Wagle, Center for South Asian Studies, University of Toronto

Photographs
AP/Wide World Photos: p. 10 (left), p. 11 (both), p. 12 (right); Piers Benatar/Panos Pictures: p. 12 (left); Bruce Coleman: p. 25 (bottom); Corbis/Magma Photo News, Inc./AFP: p. 4 (right), p. 9 (right), p. 10 (right), p. 15 (left), p. 17 (right); Corbis/Magma Photo News, Inc./Jonathan Blair: p. 27 (bottom); Corbis/Magma Photo News, Inc./Bennett Dean, Eye Ubiquitous: p. 23 (bottom); Corbis/Magma Photo News, Inc./John R. Jones, Papilio: p. 26 (left); Corbis/Magma Photo News, Inc./Ed Kashi: cover; Corbis/Magma Photo News, Inc./Christine Osborne: p. 3, p. 22 (bottom); Corbis/Magma Photo News, Inc./Galen Rowell: p. 24 (left), p. 26 (right); Corbis/Magma Photo News, Inc./Arthur Thévenart: p. 8 (bottom), p. 22 (top); Corbis/Magma Photo News, Inc./Nik Wheeler: p. 23 (top); Christine Dameyer: p. 9 (left); Ric Ergenbright: p. 25 (top); Alain Evrard/Photo Researchers: p. 5; Robert Harding: p. 4 (left), p. 21 (top), p. 24 (right), p. 29; Jim Holmes/Axiom Photographic Agency: p. 14; Ed Kashi: p. 13 (left); S. Kay/Life File: p. 27 (top); Christine Osborne: title page, p. 6 (both), p. 7 (top), p. 8 (top), p. 13 (right), p. 15 (right), p. 16, p. 18 (left), p. 21 (bottom); Trip/ B. Crawshaw: p. 7 (bottom); Trip/F. Good: p. 17 (left); Trip/ P. Kerry: p. 28 (left); Trip/Trip: p. 18 (right); p. 19 (both), p. 20 (both), p. 28 (right)

Illustrations
Dianne Eastman: icon
Alexei Mezentzev: pp. 30–31
David Wysotski, Allure Illustrations: back cover

Cover: The marble domes of the Badshahi Mosque, in the eastern city of Lahore, can be seen from a great distance. Thousands of people gather every day to pray in the courtyard, which is the largest of any mosque in the world.

Title page: Musicians from the Hunza Valley, in northern Pakistan, play drums and flutes to celebrate *Eid ul-Fitar*. During this holiday, people visit family and friends, exchange gifts, and eat delicious meals.

Icon: The Faisal Mosque, which appears at the head of each section, is in Pakistan's capital, Islamabad. It is one of the largest mosques in the world, with room for 100,000 worshipers.

Back cover: The Indus River dolphin is one of the few freshwater dolphins in the world, and it lives only in Pakistan. This species of dolphin swims on its side, which allows it to swim in shallow parts of the Indus River.

Published by
Crabtree Publishing Company

PMB 16A,
350 Fifth Avenue
Suite 3308
New York
N.Y. 10118

612 Welland Avenue
St. Catharines
Ontario, Canada
L2M 5V6

73 Lime Walk
Headington
Oxford OX3 7AD
United Kingdom

Cataloging in Publication Data
Black, Carolyn.
    Pakistan. The culture / Carolyn Black.
        p. cm. -- (Lands, peoples, and cultures series)
Includes index.
Summary: Text and photos show how the people of Pakistan, a predominantly Muslim country, celebrate holidays and festivals, using art, music, dance, and stories.
    ISBN 0-7787-9348-6 (rlb. : alk. paper) -- ISBN 0-7787-9716-3 (pb. : alk. paper)
 1. Pakistan--Civilization--Juvenile literature. [1.Pakistan--Civilization. 2. Pakistan--Social life and customs.] I. Title. II. Series.
    DS393.8 .B549 2003
    954--dc21   2002013740
                                                                LC

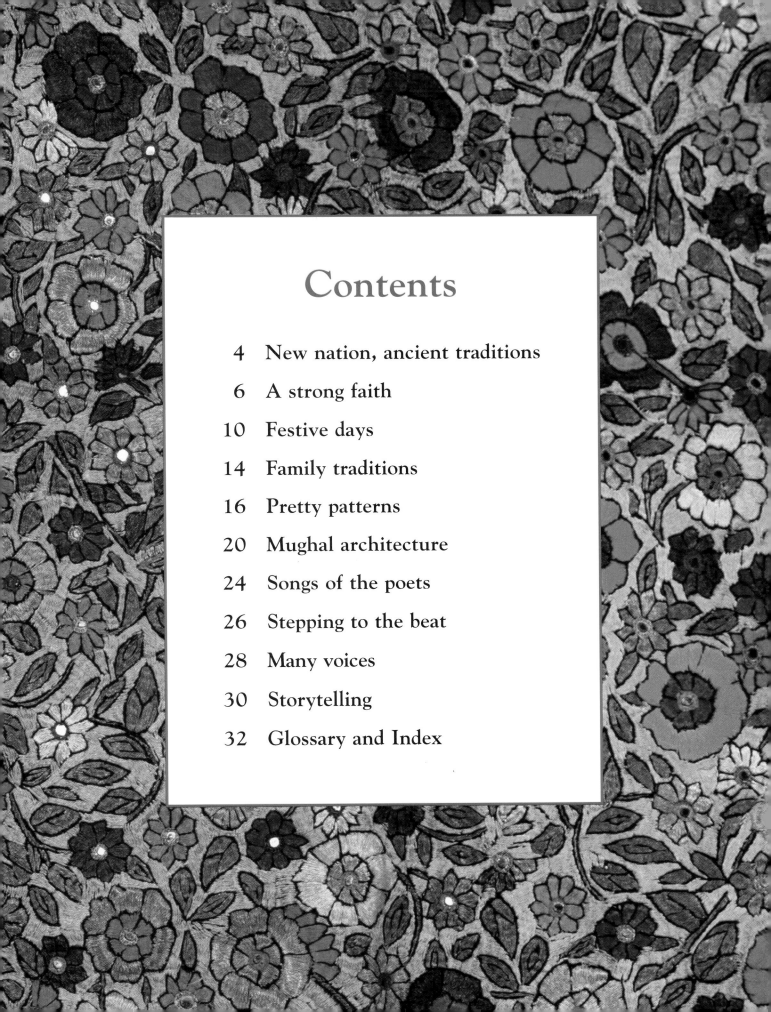

Contents

4   New nation, ancient traditions

6   A strong faith

10 Festive days

14 Family traditions

16 Pretty patterns

20 Mughal architecture

24 Songs of the poets

26 Stepping to the beat

28 Many voices

30 Storytelling

32 Glossary and Index

If you look up in most cities in Pakistan, you will see large, rounded domes rising between the other buildings. These domes are the tops of **mosques**, where Muslims pray. Most Pakistanis are Muslims. They practice the religion of Islam. Religion was the main reason for Pakistan's creation in 1947, when it split away from India to become a **homeland** for Muslims. Although Pakistan was a new country, Muslims had lived in the region for hundreds of years. They shaped the beliefs and traditions of Pakistan. Today, Islam is still an important part of life in Pakistan. Many Muslims pray at mosques five times a day, and their religion guides the music they listen to, the food they eat, the art they create, and the festivals they celebrate.

Colorful tile panels decorate the brickwork of the Wazir Khan Mosque in Lahore, in eastern Pakistan.

(opposite) The Chauburji Monument in Lahore was once the entrance to a royal garden, built in 1627 for a Mughal princess.

(above) Worshipers dance at the shrine of the Sufi saint Hazrat Shah Abdul Latif Bari Imam to celebrate the anniversary of his death. Bari Imam helped the poor and homeless people of Pakistan.

Almost all Pakistanis — about 97 percent of the population — are Muslims. Muslims believe in one God, Allah. They believe that Allah's word was revealed to the **prophet** Muhammad by an angel named Jibril, or Gabriel. These revelations are written in the *Qur'an*, the Muslim holy book. People in Pakistan who are not Muslims practice religions such as Christianity, Hinduism, Buddhism, and Zoroastrianism.

Haraam and *halaal*

At a very young age, Muslim children learn what the *Qur'an* allows and does not allow. Things that are not allowed are considered *haraam*, while things that are allowed are considered *halaal*. For instance, Muslims are not allowed to drink alcohol, so alcohol is *haraam*. The meat of most animals, except for pigs, is *halaal*, but only under certain conditions. The butcher must kill the animal in a specific way, and before he kills it, he must say the word *"bismillah,"* which means "in the name of Allah." The butcher slaughters the animal in Allah's name because Muslims believe that only Allah has the power to take away life.

Pakistanis on **hajj** *board a ship in Karachi's port, on the Arabian Sea. Every year, more than 50,000 Pakistanis leave on* **hajj**.

Muslim prayers are chanted in several positions, including standing, bowing, and kneeling with the forehead touching the ground.

Five pillars of faith

Muslims are guided by five rules called the "five pillars of faith":
1. They must believe in one God, Allah, and his prophet, Muhammad.
2. They must pray five times a day.
3. They must share their money with those in need.
4. They must fast during the Muslim month of *Ramadan*.
5. They must make a journey, called the *hajj*, to the holy city of Mecca, where Muhammad was born, at least once in their lifetime if they are healthy and able to afford the trip.

Call to prayer

Five times a day, an announcement is made from mosques across Pakistan: "God is most great. There is no God but Allah, and Muhammad is God's prophet. Come to prayer, come to security. God is most great." This announcement, known as the *azan*, lets Muslims know that it is time to pray. Traditionally, a person called a *muezzin* loudly proclaimed the *azan* from a mosque's tall, needle-thin minaret, or tower. Today, the *muezzin* usually speaks through a loudspeaker, or a recording is played. Prayer times are dawn, noon, mid-afternoon, right after sunset, and before bedtime.

The **muezzin** *must stand facing Mecca while reciting the* **azan**, *the call to prayer. He also follows the tradition of placing his fingers in his ears, so he can speak as loudly as possible without hurting his ears.*

Facing Mecca

When Pakistanis hear the *azan*, they go to a mosque or pray wherever they are. Some schools and offices have special prayer rooms. Many women pray at home because not all mosques allow women inside. Some mosques that do allow women have separate areas where they pray. Friday, or *Juma*, is the holiest day of the week. Offices, factories, and businesses close at noon and stay closed for the rest of the day so people can attend mosque to say special *Juma* prayers.

Before praying, Muslims wash their face and hands and make sure their clothes are clean. They turn toward Mecca, the city in Saudi Arabia, to pray. Most hotel rooms in Pakistan have a small arrow on the ceiling or on the furniture that points to Mecca so Muslim travelers know which way to face when praying.

Many mosques and shrines have fountains or pools of water outside for ceremonial washing before prayers.

Young men read small, illustrated versions of the **Qur'an** *outside the Data Durbar Mosque in Lahore.*

Sunnis and Shias

More than 70 groups, or sects, of Muslims exist in Pakistan, but most belong to the Sunni or Shia branch of Islam. About 77 percent of Muslims in Pakistan are Sunnis, while 20 percent are Shias. The two groups share many of the same beliefs, but Sunnis elect religious leaders, called caliphs, while Shias believe that only Muhammad's **descendants** can be true representatives of Allah on earth. They call these representatives *imams*.

A large sect of Shias, called the "Twelvers," believe that the last, or twelfth, *imam* disappeared in the 800s and has been kept alive for hundreds of years by Allah. They believe that someday he will show himself, battle evil, and bring peace to the world. Sunnis also have *imams*, but their role is different than that of Shia *imams*. Sunni *imams* are religious leaders who guide people in prayer.

Ismailis are a small sect of Shias who believe that Muhammad's descendants are still alive. Ismailis call their *imam* the Aga Khan. Prince Karim Aga Khan, who was born in 1936, lives in France, near Paris. In addition to being the Ismaili religious leader, his foundation, the Aga Khan Foundation, gives money to communities around the world, especially in Africa and Asia. This money helps build irrigation systems in small villages, and is used to build and run hospitals, schools, and mosques.

The Dai Anga Mosque in Lahore was built in 1635 for a member of the royal household of the emperor Shah Jahan, who cared for the emperor as a child.

Many people visit the shrines of Sufi saints. Sufi saints helped the poor and taught people about Islam.

Buddhism and Zoroastrianism

Small groups of Buddhists live in Pakistan, mainly in the northern area of Baltistan. They believe in reincarnation, like Hindus, and follow the teachings of a prince named Siddhartha Gautama. Gautama came to be known as "the Buddha," which means "the Enlightened One."

In the eastern city of Lahore and the southern city of Karachi, small communities of people called Parsees practice Zoroastrianism. Zoroastrianism was founded in the sixth or seventh century B.C. Parsees believe in one god, Ahura Mazda, who is symbolized by fire. Fires always burn in Parsee temples in his honor.

Christians worship at St. Patrick Catholic Church in downtown Karachi.

Shrines and saints

Sufis are Muslims who believe they can become closer to Allah through **reflection**, music, and poetry. Sufism began in the 700s, but only a few Sufis still live in Pakistan. Some early Sufis, called saints or *pirs*, had reputations as miracle workers. In Pakistan, **shrines** are often built around the tombs of *pirs*. Hundreds of people gather at the shrines, often on Thursday evenings, to pray for spiritual guidance or for help solving problems. They place rose or marigold garlands over the tombs, recite the *Qur'an*, and sing religious songs. Others make wishes and attach padlocks to the grills of the shrines. If their wishes are granted, they unlock the padlocks.

Christianity and Hinduism

About three percent of Pakistanis are not Muslims. Many are Christians. They follow the teachings of Jesus Christ, who they believe was God's son on earth. Other people, mostly in the province of Sind, practice Hinduism. They worship one creator power named Brahman and many gods and goddesses whom they consider different forms of Brahman. They also believe that people are reincarnated, or born again and again until they are free from evil.

Muslim holidays follow the lunar calendar. The lunar calendar has twelve months. Each month begins when a new moon appears, and lasts for 29 or 30 days. A year according to the lunar calendar is about ten days shorter than a year on the western calendar. This means that a month, such as *Ramadan*, might fall in winter one year and in summer many years later.

Ramadan

One of the pillars of Islam decrees that Muslims must fast, or go without food and drink, from sunrise to sunset during the month of *Ramadan*. It was during this month that Muhammad received Allah's teachings from the angel Jibril.

During *Ramadan*, people make a special effort to be truthful, tolerant, peaceful, and generous. They want their fasts, which teach them self-discipline and help them understand what it is like to go hungry, to be acceptable to Allah. Very young children, pregnant women, travelers, and sick people are not expected to fast, although older children sometimes fast for part of the day. When children are twelve years old, they begin fasting for the whole month of *Ramadan*. A child's first fast is an important event.

Muslims gather at a mosque in Lahore to break the **Ramadan** *fast with a special meal called* **iftaar**. *Going without food or water during the day is hard on people's bodies. To make fasting easier, offices, shops, and factories close in the afternoon so people can go home to rest.*

Breaking the fast

Each night of *Ramadan*, people break the fast by eating a date and drinking some water. After prayers, they eat a special meal called *iftaar*. Families and friends visit one another for *iftaar*, or people feast on food bought from street stalls. Near the end of the month, streets become even busier as preparations for the celebration of *Eid ul-Fitar*, which marks the end of *Ramadan*, begin. People flock to **bazaars** and shopping centers to purchase new clothes, jewelry, and food for the *Eid ul-Fitar* meal.

Two friends exchange greetings of **"Eid mubarak,"** *or* **"Eid** *greetings," outside a mosque in Karachi.*

Eid ul-Fitar

Eid ul-Fitar, or "the Festival of Fast Breaking," begins the day after the new moon appears. No one is sure exactly when that will be, so on the 28th, 29th, and 30th nights of *Ramadan*, children rush onto rooftops to check the sky. On the morning of the festival, people dress up in new clothes and go to the mosque for morning prayers. So many people attend morning prayers that mosques in cities overflow, and people pray on the streets and in parks.

Family and friends drop by one another's homes all day with cakes and candies. They eat special foods such as *sawayan*, a sweet dish made with long, thin noodles, milk, almonds, pistachios, and dried fruit. *Eid ul-Fitar* is a day for giving. People exchange gifts and give money, called *fitrana*, to poor people. They also donate money to charities, older children give money to their younger brothers and sisters, and children receive money from adults.

Children receive money as gifts during **Eid ul-Fitar**. *These children spend their money on colorful balloons at this* **Eid ul-Fitar** *fair.*

After a month of fasting from sunrise to sunset, Muslims in Pakistan prepare for **Eid ul-Fitar** *by stocking up on food and gifts in marketplaces, such as this one in Lahore.*

11

Animals chosen for sacrifice for **Eid ul-Azha** *are first decorated with colorful fabric, flowers, and tinsel.*

Eid ul-Azha

Pakistanis celebrate *Eid ul-Azha*, "the Festival of the Sacrifice," on the tenth day of the last lunar month, *Zul-Hijja*. On this day, and for three days after, they remember a holy story about the prophet Abraham, who was willing to sacrifice his son because Allah told him to do it. Just as Abraham was about to kill his son, Allah was so pleased with his obedience that he allowed Abraham to sacrifice a sheep instead. During *Eid ul-Azha*, people remember Allah's mercy by sacrificing an animal. They visit local markets to choose a fat goat, cow, or sheep, whose wool is sometimes dyed pink, green, or blue to attract customers. After they sacrifice the animal, the meat is cut into three equal portions: one for the family, one for relatives, and one for the poor.

Muharram

The festival of *Muharram* lasts for 40 days, beginning on the first day of the first month, also called *Muharram*. During *Muharram*, Muslims mourn the brutal killing of Imam Hussain, Muhammad's grandson, and male members of his family, including many young children. They were killed 1,300 years ago during a battle with another group of Muslims.

Sunnis and Shias mourn Hussain's death in different ways. Sunnis do not play music or dance for the first ten days of *Muharram*. It was on the tenth day, known as *Ashura*, that Hussain was killed. Shias do not wear jewelry for the whole holiday, and they do not allow any celebrations, such as marriage. They perform plays that depict the events leading to Hussain's death, and listen to religious scholars, called *ulemas*, read from the *Qur'an*. For Shias, the main part of the celebration takes part on *Ashura*, when they walk through the streets in large **processions**.

During **Muharram** *processions, some young men volunteer to beat their backs with whips and chains that have five short, sharp blades at the ends. They do this to understand the suffering of Imam Hussain.*

Melas

Pakistanis love to visit the fairs, or *melas*, that take place in different parts of the country throughout the year. Many *melas* celebrate harvests or the coming of spring. Markets become busier, traveling circuses with dancing bears and monkeys appear, and people set up merry-go-rounds, swings, and slides in town or village squares.

In February, at a *mela* in Lahore, the best cattle, sheep, buffalo, bulls, and camels are brought from all over Pakistan to compete for trophies. They are led in parades by their owners, who wear the traditional dress of their region.

A crowd gathers to watch traditional horse dancing at the Sibi Camel Festival, in the province of Baluchistan. The festival also includes camel racing, animal markets, and displays of crafts and dancing.

Urs

The biggest *melas*, called *urs*, take place at the shrines of Sufi saints. Many villages in Pakistan have their own small shrine, dedicated to a local saint. The *urs* commemorates the anniversary of the saint's death. Thousands of people pray at the shrine, where colored tents, jugglers, snake charmers, palm readers, and even fortune tellers whose parrots select people's fortunes from a deck of cards add to the festivities.

An imam *prays at a shrine during an* urs *celebration. Before the celebration begins, the shrine is washed and decorated with fresh flowers.*

Basant

At the beginning of March, colorful kites soar through the sky above Lahore. The festival of *Basant* marks the coming of spring. From fields, streets, and even flat rooftops, people take part in kite-flying competitions. They try to cut the strings of their competitors' kites with their kite strings, which have tiny bits of glass glued to them. When a string is cut, drums and trumpets signal that another competitor is out. Children run through the streets to catch the cut kites, sometimes climbing trees and telephone poles to retrieve them.

Family traditions

*A young girl carefully reads the **Qur'an**. When she has read all 30 chapters, her proud parents will invite relatives and friends to a celebratory feast.*

Hospitality is very important to Pakistanis. Some families have special rooms in their homes where they receive guests, and many families give visitors small gifts, such as pieces of cloth. Pakistanis are especially generous during family celebrations, when relatives, friends, and neighbors are invited to share happy events.

A new baby

When a baby is born, the father sends colorful boxes packed with sweets, called *laddus*, to friends and relatives. Traditionally, some families also gave babies something sweet to taste. They would rub foods such as crushed dates or sugar on their gums or tongues in the hope that the babies would grow up to be sweet. To protect babies from harm, mothers sometimes give their children good luck charms, called *ta'weez*. *Ta'weez* are **amulets** with verses from the *Qur'an*.

Muslims believe that one of the most important gifts they give their babies is a name. When a baby is seven days old, the family holds an *aqeeqa* ceremony. The baby is named and its hair is shaved off. Traditionally, wealthy families weighed the hair and gave its weight in gold or silver to the poor. The family also sacrifices goats or sheep to Allah, in thanks, and gives the meat to the poor. Then, they hold a feast for relatives and friends.

Learning the *Qur'an*

Religious education is important for Muslim children. Only a few hours after a baby is born, the *azan* is whispered in his or her ear. Before some children are even one year old, their parents teach them to hold up one finger and say the phrase "Allah *eik*," which means "There is only one Allah." Between the ages of four and six, the family holds a *bismillah* ceremony, at which a religious scholar called a *mullah* asks the child to say the word "*bismillah*," which is the first word in the *Qur'an*. The *mullah* also teaches the child to write the first letter of the Arabic alphabet, the language in which the *Qur'an* is written. For many months after the ceremony, the child learns to read Arabic so he or she can read from the *Qur'an*.

Before the **nikah,** *or wedding ceremony,* **mehndi** *is used to paint a bride's hands and feet with beautiful floral designs.* **Mehndi** *is a dark red paste made from crushed henna leaves, cloves, and black tea.*

Weddings

In Pakistan, parents often choose their children's husbands or wives, but usually a formal arrangement is not made until the couple agrees to the wedding. At the ceremony, or *nikah*, the bride and groom verbally agree to the marriage and sign papers in front of an *imam*. The bride wears a heavily embroidered, colorful dress and a lot of jewelry. She and the groom sometimes drink almond-flavored milk from the same glass and feed one another sweets to guarantee a sweet and healthy life together. Traditionally, especially if the bride and groom had never seen one another before the wedding, they were given a mirror to see themselves together, as a couple.

After the *nikah*, the couple, their families, and guests attend an elaborate feast. Then, the couple goes to their new home, where the bride's dowry awaits them. Traditionally, the dowry, which was a gift from the bride's parents, was jewelry and clothes. Now, refrigerators and TVs are just as common.

Burial

When a Muslim dies, family and friends go to the dead person's home to pray and mourn beside the body. The body is bathed, wrapped in a white cloth, and sprinkled with rose petals. After the person is buried, the grave is marked with two low stones: one for the feet and one for the head.

The Parsees believe that **cremation** and burial pollute the sky and earth, so they place their dead in tall towers called "towers of silence." Vultures and crows fly into the open tops of the towers and eat the bodies.

Only men carry the body of a person who died to the burial grounds because many Muslims believe that women, who bear life, should not visit places of death.

15

Hundreds of years ago, most Muslim artists did not draw or paint living creatures. They thought that creating people or animals in art showed disrespect to Allah, who they believed was the only creator of life. These artists found other ways to produce beautiful art. On tiles and pottery, they painted intricate patterns made of repeating geometric shapes. In other patterns, called arabesques, curving lines formed flowers, leaves, and fruit. Today, Pakistani artists still use these ancient patterns to decorate the insides of mosques, as well as handicrafts. Creating handicrafts, such as carpets, pottery, and leather shoes, is part of everyday life for many Pakistanis, who earn a living by selling their work.

Pottery

Potters across Pakistan shape sticky pieces of clay into plates, pots, and vases, which they bake in hot ovens to harden and dry. Skillful potters in Bahawalpur, in the province of Punjab, produce a delicate, black pottery called *kaghazi*, which is as thin as paper. Some potters use a technique that is more than 1,000 years old to decorate their work. They paint crisscrossing lines on the baked clay, and then paint over the lines with transparent glazes of different colors to make the objects shine. Other potters decorate their work with paintings of flowers and animals, such as leopards, bulls, and rhinoceroses.

(top) The ancient city of Multan, in the province of Punjab, is famous for its tilework. Glittering blue and white tiles decorate the mausoleum, or burial place, of the Sufi saint Rukn-i-Alam.

16

The art of writing

Elaborate writing, called calligraphy, decorates colorful tiles and long **scrolls** in Pakistan's mosques. Calligraphers copy passages of the *Qur'an*, the name of Allah, or his 99 qualities, or names, using brushes and paints, or pens and inks of different colors. Often, they surround the passages with arabesques and other designs. Early calligraphers cut their own pens from tall, hollow grasses. Good pens were valued and passed down for generations, or they were buried with the calligraphers when they died.

Carpets must be cleaned before they are sold. These carpets have been cleaned at a factory in Peshawar, in the North-West Frontier Province, and then spread on planks of wood to dry in the sun.

Making carpets

Pakistan's handmade carpets are popular throughout the world. To make a carpet, thousands of wool or silk threads in different colors are tied together with tiny knots to create wavy lines, flowers, and other designs. Pictures of rows of camels march across carpets made in the dry province of Baluchistan, where many people ride the animals. Stripes and geometric shapes decorate traditional Sind carpets, called *farashi* rugs, which are woven from camel hair, wool, and cotton.

Large carpets take about ten months to make and are very expensive to buy. Many carpets are made by young children, whose small, nimble fingers are good at tying tiny knots. These children work long hours in carpet factories, making little money. People also make carpets in their homes. Sometimes, the whole family joins in the work. They sell their carpets to carpet factories or at bazaars.

Panels of delicate calligraphy appear on the walls of the Wazir Khan Mosque in Lahore.

Colorful embroidery, small mirrors, and patterns of shells and beads decorate clothing in Baluchistan.

Needle and thread

Pakistani tailors embroider shirts, hats, and even shoes with designs made of cotton, silk, or wool threads. Women in the Hunza Valley, in northern Pakistan, embroider almost anything they can pull a needle through, including bookmarks, wall hangings, picture frames, evening bags, and wallets. Fancier embroidery shimmers with gold and silver threads, but the embroidery that sparkles the most is combined with *shisha*, or the art of sewing tiny mirrors into clothes, hats, wall hangings, and picture frames.

Many craftspeople in Peshawar use brass to create household items and decorative objects. In the Hindko language, spoken in Peshawar, the word for brass is **mis***, and artists who work with brass are called* **misgar***. The Misgaran Bazaar is a large marketplace where craftspeople sell beautiful brass cooking utensils, plates, and other objects.*

Metalwork

Goldsmiths and silversmiths create elegant jewelry like that worn by the Mughals, the Muslims who ruled Pakistan more than 400 years ago. Rubies, emeralds, and pearls adorn gold bracelets, earrings, and chokers. In northern Pakistan, silver bracelets are decorated with a bright blue stone called lapis lazuli.

Other metalworkers make plates, teapots, vases, and other household items from copper and brass. They engrave dainty designs into the metal with sharp tools and a small hammer. The most popular designs are twisting vines with flowers. In Punjab, people lay strips of gold and silver into metal items. This technique is called damascening. Punjabis also decorate brass and copper with filigree, or fine wires of gold, silver, and copper. Fancy filigree designs appear on window frames and folding screens.

Painting

During the rule of the Mughal emperors, miniature paintings became popular. In the 1500s, war scenes, ceremonies at the palace, legends, and royal hunts often appeared on the tiny paintings. Later miniatures had animals, flowers, and trees. The paint was made of water mixed with crushed insects, earth, or rare stones. When a Mughal emperor liked the work of a painter of miniatures, he might reward the artist with a luxurious robe, an elephant, land, or even a village.

In the 1900s, Pakistani painters were influenced by European art. Shakir Ali (1916–1975) painted in a style called cubism, where objects look as if they are broken into pieces and stuck back together again. Ali mixed the bodies of women and animals in his paintings, including the series *Leda and the Swan*. Another painter, Unver Shafi (1961–), uses the strange shapes of abstract art to tell about his society. In his painting *Burqa*, the folds in a headscarf worn by a woman take up the whole canvas.

The details of a miniature painting are so tiny that the paintbrushes needed to create them were sometimes made with one hair of a squirrel's tail or one cat whisker. The ancient art of miniature painting is still being taught and practiced in Pakistan today.

Abdur Rahman Chughtai

Abdur Rahman Chughtai (1894–1975) is considered Pakistan's greatest painter. During his life, he finished almost 2,000 **watercolors**, thousands of pencil sketches and miniatures, and nearly 300 etchings and aquatints, which are prints that look like watercolors but are made using a copper plate. Although watercolors and etchings are not Pakistani artforms, Chughtai combined them with the Pakistani culture by adding geometric and floral patterns. He also painted many portraits, an artform traditionally not allowed by Islam.

*Sadequain (1930–1987), one of Pakistan's best known artists, painted scenes from the **Qur'an** and from poems, including those of Urdu poet Faiz Ahmed Faiz.*

19

Mughal architecture

In 1525, a Muslim from Central Asia invaded the area now called Pakistan. His name was Babur, and he founded the Mughal dynasty, a family of powerful and wealthy Muslim emperors who ruled the entire Indian **subcontinent** for the next 200 years. The Mughals paid **architects** to build majestic forts, palaces, and mosques across the land that they ruled. Many of these buildings still stand in Pakistan. Their large domes, slim towers, and pointed archways continue to influence architects in the country.

Lahore Fort

The Mughal emperor Akbar made Lahore his capital city between 1584 and 1598. He rebuilt an earlier fort and constructed many new buildings inside. Lahore Fort includes the gleaming, white marble Moti Masjid, or Pearl Mosque, and the Diwan-e-Aam, or Hall of Public Audience. Here, the emperor made a daily public appearance, received important visitors, and watched military parades.

Shish Mahal

Shish Mahal, in the Lahore Fort, is also known as the Palace of Mirrors. It was built by Shah Jahan in 1631 as a home for the empress and her court. The walls and high roofs of the Shish Mahal are covered with thousands of tiny mirrors that create beautiful patterns. Today, visitors to the Shish Mahal take candles into its domed rooms to watch light dance over the mirrors.

(above) The ceiling of the Shish Mahal displays the artform of **shishgari,** *which is traditional in Punjab.* **Shishgari** *uses hundreds of thousands of tiny mirror fragments to create mosaics.*

(left) The original walls of Lahore Fort were made of mud, but they were later replaced by sturdier brick walls. Moats, which are ditches filled with water, once surrounded the fort, to further protect royalty living inside.

Badshahi Mosque

The Badshahi Mosque, which is also in Lahore Fort, was completed in 1676 during the rule of Mughal emperor Aurangzeb. Four minarets made of red sandstone rise from a roof with three marble domes. The rooms above the huge entrance gate are not open to the public. It is said that they hold the hairs of the prophet Muhammad, as well as items that belonged to his daughter Fatima and her husband, Ali.

The Badshahi Mosque, which means "the King's Mosque," has 22 red sandstone steps leading up to the main entrance. The enormous courtyard holds between 60,000 and 100,000 people.

Shalimar Gardens

Just outside Lahore, the Shalimar Gardens offer visitors a relaxing place to rest or stroll. Shah Jahan designed the gardens around a white marble palace, using waterfalls, large square pools, and more than 400 fountains to create a peaceful and cool setting. Canals run through the two main gardens. Each garden was designed with three levels, so people on the lowest level would not see people on the highest level. It is thought that women in the emperor's family used the highest level.

The Ravi River feeds pools, canals, and fountains in the Shalimar Gardens. The river's water also irrigates the garden's many flowerbeds.

The tomb of Bibi Jawindi is a well-known landmark in the eastern town of Uch, in Punjab. Bibi Jawindi was famous for her strong religious beliefs, in addition to being the great-granddaughter of a Sufi saint.

Shah Jahan Mosque

Gold-colored stonework, blue and patterned tiles, and calligraphy decorate the inside of the Shah Jahan Mosque in the town of Thatta, in Sind. Designed by Shah Jahan's architects, the mosque was built between 1644 and 1647. Some people say that Shah Jahan built the mosque because the people of Thatta sheltered him after he angered his father. Other people say that Shah Jahan wanted to thank the townspeople for helping him win the war for the throne after his father's death.

Several Mughal dynasties ruled in the town of Thatta, creating many impressive monuments. The Shah Jahan Mosque has 93 domes, specially designed to carry the voice of the imam leading the prayers.

Building a dream

More than 100,000 artists and craftspeople worked on the Bhong Mosque between 1932 and 1980. A landowner named Rais Ghazi Muhammad had the mosque built in Bhong, Punjab, using a mixture of artistic styles. He combined traditional elements, such as glazed tiles, **frescoes**, gold leaf, painted and stained-glass windows, carved white marble, and calligraphy, with modern elements, including colorful cement tiles and wrought iron. People say that Ghazi Muhammad got the idea for his mosque in a dream. He also dreamed that if he stopped working on the mosque, he would die. According to legend, he died one week after the mosque was completed.

(above) The Quaid-e-Azam Mausoleum, in Karachi, holds the body of Muhammad Ali Jinnah (1875–1948), the founder of Pakistan and its first governor general.

(below) Many artistic styles appear on the Bhong Mosque, including colored tiles applied in a patchwork pattern.

(above) During the time of the British Raj, or rule, some types of British music and instruments were brought to Pakistan. This musician plays the traditional Scottish bagpipes, and wears a uniform with a draping of Scottish tartan, or plaid cloth.

Pakistan's early poetry, especially the religious poetry of Sufi saints, has inspired music that is popular today. Contemporary musicians give traditional, religious songs a modern twist by speeding them up, changing the lyrics, or combining them with electric guitars and electronic keyboards.

A poetic tradition

In the 700s, Sufi saints began writing religious poetry and turning it into song. They believed that performing and listening to music brought them closer to Allah. Their songs were about the pain of separation from Allah and the joy of believing in him. Some songs told of romances and folktales. Two of Pakistan's most famous Sufi poets were Lal Shahbaz Qalandar (1177–1274) and Shah Abdul Latif (1689–1752).

Between the 1500s and 1700s, thousands of poets from across Pakistan wrote religious poems in their regional languages. Poets who wrote in Urdu, now Pakistan's national language, recited poetry about their love for Allah and romantic love at outdoor recitals called *mushairah*. Poets in Pakistan and northern India still recite their work at *mushairah*, which often attract as many people as sporting events do.

*(below) A musician plays a traditional stringed instrument called a **dhambiro**, which is made from the wood of the tamarisk tree.*

Qawwali

Traditionally, *qawwali* singers, or *qawwals*, chanted religious phrases from Sufi songs, accompanied by a *sarangi*. A *sarangi* is a hollow wooden instrument with strings, and is played with a bow. Since the *sarangi* takes up to half an hour to retune between songs, many modern musicians play a harmonium, a cross between an organ and an accordion, instead. *Qawwali* songs can be very long. Many last fifteen minutes and some last more than half an hour.

Modern *qawwals* perform with bands, called "parties." Each party has a lead singer, a few main backup singers, and a chorus of singers who repeat the *qawwal*'s chant and clap their hands. These bands perform the songs of Sufi saints and songs that they write. One of the most famous modern *qawwals* was Nusrat Fateh Ali Khan (1948–1997). He sang a wide range of notes with faster and more complicated rhythms than those used in traditional *qawwali* songs.

The people of the Kalash Valley, in the North-West Frontier Province, play music to accompany their many folk dances. Music and dances are often performed at harvest festivals, where drums of different sizes keep the beat.

Musicians in Gilgit play flutes to celebrate the festival of **Nauroz,** *which welcomes the beginning of spring in* **March. Nauroz** *is celebrated only by people in the north.*

Ghazal

Qawwals sometimes perform a slow, emotional song called a *ghazal*. This rhyming song developed from classical Arabic love poetry. Common themes include longing, frustration, love that is not returned, and madness, as well as religious devotion. *Ghazal* singers are accompanied by long-necked stringed instruments called *sitars*, drums called *tablas*, and violins, playing sad music in the background.

Stepping to the beat

(above) The Kalasha have special dances for men, women, and children, which are performed separately. Kalasha women dance in a circle with their hands around each other's shoulders.

Pakistanis celebrate special occasions, such as harvest festivals, with lively dances. Some dances symbolize the defeat of evil, while others involve playful games. People in every region of Pakistan have their own dances, which their **ancestors** performed hundreds of years ago.

Khattak

The Khattak, a people who live in the North-West Frontier Province, perform a special dance that is named after their tribe. Traditionally, the *khattak* was a military dance, in which men danced in a circle, holding swords, guns, or handkerchiefs to show their courage and desire to go into battle. Today, the *khattak* is danced at celebrations, with men still holding guns, which they sometimes fire into the air. The firings are in time to the music of shrill flutes called *surnai* and pounding drums, such as the large *dhol*. The dancers wear white, short skirts over white pants, along with colorful embroidered vests.

Bhangra

For years, young men in Punjabi villages have danced the *bhangra* to celebrate the harvest. Dancers circle around a musician who beats out exciting rhythms on a *dhol* or other drum. At first, the drum beats slowly and the dancers move only their feet. As the drum beats faster and faster, the dancers whirl, bend, hop on one foot, and clap or snap their fingers. During all this activity, they find time to recite funny poems and rhyming verses two lines long, known as *bolis*. Young people in Pakistan's cities dance the *bhangra* at clubs, to the rhythm of *bhangra* music mixed with techno music.

(below) Dancers near Pakistan's border with Afghanistan perform a traditional dance that imitates battles with swords.

26

"The Stick Dance" is a Baluchi dance performed in a circle. Dancers each carry two sticks, which they tap together or against other dancers' sticks while moving to the music.

"Wake up!"

On the night before a wedding, women in Punjabi villages who are related to the groom sing and dance the *jaago* through the streets and in people's homes. *Jaago* means "wake up." It also refers to the large clay or copper pot that the women take turns carrying on their heads. The pot is decorated with as many as 30 candles. The light is meant to wake up the villagers so they can celebrate the upcoming wedding with the dancers. The women knock on people's doors. When they are let inside, they dance in a circle and sing songs about the village. Sometimes, they also tease people in the room by singing about them or imitating them in a dance.

A groom in traditional wedding dress performs a dance with his brother, in Nagar, a town in the Northern Areas.

Dancing with camels

People in the Cholistan Desert, in eastern Punjab, perform a folkdance called the *jhumar* at *melas,* or fairs. Both men and women move in a graceful circle around a campfire. Trained camels take turns dancing by lifting their legs and moving in step to a loud drum beat. Like the men and women, the camels wear silver jewelry that tinkles with every step.

Two friends chat in Punjabi while drinking a cup of tea.

Before Pakistan became a country in 1947, the British ruled the Indian subcontinent for about 200 years. They used English as the language of government and education. Today, Pakistanis who work in large businesses or for the government speak English, and English is the country's official language. Pakistan's national language is Urdu, which developed from a combination of Sanskrit, Persian, Arabic, and Turkic. Major newspapers are either in English or Urdu, and children learn both languages at school.

The language that children learn first, before they go to school, is often not English or Urdu, but a **dialect** of the language spoken in their region. More than 300 dialects of about two dozen languages exist in Pakistan, and many Pakistanis speak more than one language. The major regional languages are Punjabi, Sindhi, Pushtu or Pashto, and Baluchi.

Urdu

Although most Pakistanis understand Urdu, only Mohajirs, or Muslims who came to Pakistan from India shortly after Pakistan's creation, speak it as their first language. Spoken Urdu is almost identical to Hindi, the language that people speak in northern India. The main difference is that complex Hindi words come from an ancient language called Sanskrit, while complex Urdu words come from ancient Persian and Arabic.

Newspapers, magazines, and books are available in both Urdu and English. Urdu letters are similar to Arabic letters and are written from right to left, instead of left to right like English and Hindi.

English	Urdu
What is your name?	*Apka nam kya hai?*
My name is ….	*Mera naam … hai.*
How are you?	*Ap khairiyat se hain?*
Everything's fine.	*Sab thik hai.*
Please.	*Mehrbanee kar kay.*
Thank you.	*Shukria.*
Hello.	*Asslaamalekum, aadab,* or *hallo.*
Goodbye.	*Khuda hafiz.*
Yes.	*Ji han.*
No.	*Ji nahin.*
What time is it?	*Kiya baja hai?*
See you again.	*Phir milenge.*

Alphabet soup

Pakistanis write their regional languages using various alphabets. People in Sind write Sindhi using a variation of the Arabic alphabet, with extra letters to represent sounds that are not in Arabic. In Pakistan, Punjabis write Punjabi using the Urdu alphabet, which is similar to the Persian and Arabic alphabets.

The Pathans, who live in the North-West Frontier Province and Baluchistan, have spoken Pushtu, or Pashto, for centuries, but until recently they had no alphabet with which to write it. Some Pathans worry that if they do not write down their language, it will disappear. Today, they are learning to write Pushtu with a version of the Persian alphabet. The **nomadic** Baluchis only began to write their language, which is related to Persian, in the 1900s, using the Persian script.

This girl is learning to read Urdu. She also learns how to speak and read English at school.

Common bonds

No matter what language Pakistanis speak, most of them understand the Arabic word *inshaallah*, or "if Allah wills." They repeat this word during the day as a reminder that only Allah has the power to control what happens. A common Arabic greeting is *"Salaam alaikum,"* which means "Peace be with you." Pakistanis who are greeted with this phrase by older people reply by repeating the phrase. To people their own age or younger, they respond with the words *"Walaikum salaam,"* meaning "And with you too." Another common word is *acha.* Depending on the tone of voice Pakistanis use, *acha* means everything from "yes," "hmm," "I agree," and "really," to "no way!"

Storytelling

People in Pakistan have told and retold folktales for generations, passing down favorites to their children, who grow up and tell them to their children. Each region has its own folktales. Some are about legendary characters or historical events. Others, such as the famous Punjabi story of Hir and Ranja, tell unhappy stories of lovers who are separated. Still others are folktales that describe the adventures of animals, and are meant to teach listeners lessons.

The farmer, the crocodile, and the jackal

There was once a sly crocodile that lived in a pond by a village. From time to time, he gobbled up the villagers. One year, a **drought** caused the pond to dry up. The crocodile, who was roasting in the sun, called out to the villagers, "Please take pity on me and show me where to find water. Otherwise, I will die in this heat."

All the villagers ignored him except for an old farmer, who felt sorry for the crocodile. He led the thirsty animal to a nearby pond with a lot of water. The crocodile took a good, long drink, and then grabbed the old farmer's leg with his teeth.

"You ungrateful beast!" cried the farmer. "Is this how you repay me for my help?"

Just then, a jackal, the smartest animal in the animal kingdom, sauntered toward the pond. The old man said, "I will tell the jackal what happened. If he decides that it is fair for you to eat me, then you shall." The crocodile let go of the man's leg and slowly shook his green, scaly head in agreement. He was secretly pleased because as soon as the jackal came near him, he would have two meals instead of just one.

The jackal listened to the man's story, keeping a safe distance from the crocodile. Afterward, he said, "To judge fairly, I need to see the dry pond." Then, he politely added, "After you, sir," to the crocodile. Once the crocodile's back was turned, the jackal whispered to the man, "You are foolish for trusting the crocodile. Now, run one way, and I'll run the other." In seconds, the crocodile had lost both his meals. He decided to take revenge on the jackal, who he knew had tricked him.

First, he crept back to the full pond and lay under the water, near the bank. Soon after, the jackal approached the pond and leaned over the water to drink. The crocodile snapped at his leg and caught it in his mouth. "You silly crocodile," exclaimed the jackal. "That is a tree root, not my leg." The crocodile let go, and the jackal ran away. The crocodile snorted in anger, but did not give up. He hid inside a pile of fruit that had fallen from the trees, leaving only his two, beady eyes sticking out. The jackal, who sniffed the fruit from far away, walked toward it with his stomach rumbling, but scampered away when he saw the crocodile's gleaming eyes. The crocodile realized that he would need help to catch the clever jackal.

One day, he saw the old farmer and said to him, "I can make you a rich man. Valuable jewels lie at the bottom of this pond. I will heap them in your lap if you catch the jackal for me."

"Easily done," said the farmer, forgetting that the jackal had saved his life.

The farmer lay down in his field as if he were dead. The jackal was hunting nearby for food. When he saw the farmer, he thought, "It looks like the farmer has died from his hard work. He would make a tasty meal." The jackal suddenly became suspicious: "What if the farmer is playing a trick to help the crocodile catch me?" To make sure that the farmer was really dead, the jackal said in a loud voice, "This can't really be a dead man. Dead men shake their legs. Only people who are alive lie still." Trying to prove he was dead, the farmer shook his legs. As soon as he did, the jackal skipped off. He had outsmarted the farmer and the crocodile. The farmer remained without jewels, and the crocodile, without his revenge.

Glossary

amulet A small piece of jewelry worn as a charm against evil

ancestor A person from whom one is descended

architect A designer of buildings

bazaar An area of small shops and stalls

cremation The practice of burning a dead person's body, usually as part of a funeral

descendant A person who can trace his or her family roots to a certain family or group

dialect A version of a language spoken in one region

drought A long period of time when no rain falls

fresco An image painted on wet plaster

homeland A country that is identified with a particular people or ethnic group

irrigation The process of supplying water to land using ditches, sprinklers, and other means

mosque A sacred building in which Muslims worship

nomadic Having no fixed home and moving from place to place in search of food and water

procession A group of persons or vehicles moving along in an orderly, formal manner

prophet A person who is believed to speak on behalf of God

reflection Concentrated thinking about a particular topic

scroll A roll of parchment, or very thin paper, with writing on it

shrine A place of worship that is connected with a certain holy person

subcontinent A large landmass that is part of a continent, but is considered independent

watercolor A painting created with paint mixed with water

Index

Ali, Shakir 19
Arabic 14, 28, 29
architecture 20–23
art 4, 16–19, 20, 22
Badshahi Mosque 21
Baluchi 28, 29
Basant 13
bhangra 26
Bhong Mosque 22
births 14
British rule 24, 28
Buddhism 6, 9
calligraphy 17, 22
carpets 16, 17
Christianity 6, 9
Chughtai, Abdur Rahman 19
dances 4, 25, 26–27
Eid ul-Azha 12
Eid ul-Fitar 11
embroidery 18

English 28
fairs 13, 27
folktales 30–31
food 10, 11, 15
forts 20–21
funerals 15
Hinduism 6, 9
holidays 10–12, 13, 25
Islam 4, 6–12, 13, 14–15, 16, 17, 19, 24, 25, 29
Ismailis 8
jaago 27
jhumar 27
Khan, Nusrat Fateh Ali 25
khattak 26
kites 13
Lahore Fort 20
languages 14, 28–29
mausoleums 16, 22, 23
mehndi 15

metalwork 18
miniatures 19
mosques 4, 7, 8, 10, 11, 17, 20, 21, 22, 23
Mughals 18, 19, 20–22
Muharram 12
music 24–25, 26, 27
musical instruments 24, 25, 26, 27
Nauroz 25
paintings 19
poetry 24, 25, 26
pottery 16
Punjabi 28, 29
Pushtu 28, 29
qawwali 25
Ramadan 10
religion 4, 6–12, 13, 14–15, 16, 17, 19, 24, 25
Sadequain 19

Shafi, Unver 19
Shah Jahan Mosque 22
Shalimar Gardens 21
Shias 8, 12
shishgari 20
Shish Mahal 20
shrines 4, 7, 9, 13
Sibi Camel Festival 13
Sindhi 28, 29
Sufi saints 4, 9, 13, 24, 25
Sunnis 8, 12
tiles 4, 16, 17, 22
Urdu 24, 28–29
urs 13
weddings 15, 27
Zoroastrianism 6, 9, 15

1 2 3 4 5 6 7 8 9 0   Printed in the USA   0 9 8 7 6 5 4 3 2